NEIL DIAMOND

**MELODY LINE, CHORDS AND LYRICS
FOR KEYBOARD • GUITAR • VOCAL**

HAL•LEONARD®

ISBN 0-7935-5257-5

HAL•LEONARD®
CORPORATION
7777 W. BLUEMOUND RD. P.O. BOX 13819 MILWAUKEE, WI 53213

Welcome to the PAPERBACK SONGS SERIES.

Do you play piano, guitar, electronic keyboard, sing or play any instrument for that matter? If so, this handy "pocket tune" book is for you.

The concise, one-line music notation consists of:

MELODY, LYRICS & CHORD SYMBOLS

Whether strumming the chords on guitar, "faking" an arrangement on piano/keyboard or singing the lyrics, these fake book style arrangements can be enjoyed at any experience level — hobbyist to professional.

The musical skills necessary to successfully use this book are minimal. If you play guitar and need some help with chords, a basic chord chart is included at the back of the book.

While playing and singing is the first thing that comes to mind when using this book, it can also serve as a compact, comprehensive reference guide.

However you choose to use this PAPERBACK SONGS SERIES book, by all means have fun!

CONTENTS

AMERICA
from the Motion Picture THE JAZZ SINGER

Words and Music by
NEIL DIAMOND

On the boats and on ___ the planes,
Got a dream to take ___ them there,

they're com - ing to A - mer - i - ca.
they're com - ing to A - mer - i - ca.

Nev - er look - ing back ___ a - gain,
Got a dream _ they've come ___ to share,

they're com - ing to A - mer - i - ca, Home,
they're com - ing to A - mer - i - ca.

don't it seem so far - a - way?

Oh, we're trav - el - ing light to - day

in the eye of the storm, ___

in the eye of the storm. _

Home, to a new and a shin -

8

9

AND THE GRASS WON'T PAY NO MIND

Words and Music by
NEIL DIAMOND

- ly fall - in' on my face _
- wet kiss - es. Your hands gen -
- ers grow - ing as you lay _

_ as in a dream. _
- tle in re - ply. _ }
_ sleep - in' in my arms.)

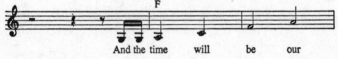

And the time will be our

time, And The Grass Won't

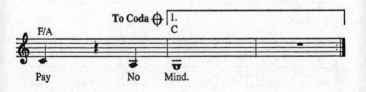

Pay No Mind.

Mind. Child, touch my soul _

12

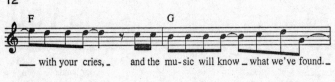

_ with your cries, _ and the mu-sic will know _ what we've found. _

_ I hear a hun -

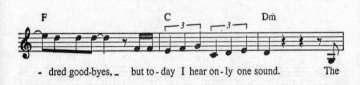

- dred good-byes, _ but to-day I hear on-ly one sound. The

mo-ment we're liv-ing is now. Na, na, na, na, _ na.

CODA

Mind. No, the

grass won't pay no mind. _

ALL I REALLY NEED IS YOU

Words by NEIL DIAMOND
Music by NEIL DIAMOND,
ALAN LINDGREN and TOM HENSLEY

14

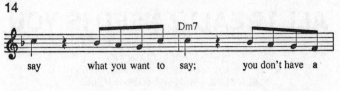

say   what you want to say;   you don't have **a**

chance in the world.   Can I,   know-in' how I've

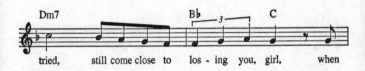

tried,   still come close to los- ing you, girl,   when

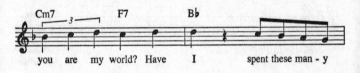

you are   my world? Have   I   spent these man - y

years   try - in' but in vain   to   tell   you?

Don't you know it, too?   All I Real - ly Need   Is

You.   *(Instrumental)*

15

AND THE SINGER SINGS HIS SONG

Words and Music by
NEIL DIAMOND

ANGEL ABOVE MY HEAD

Words and Music by
NEIL DIAMOND

Moderately

If you're gon-na be true to me,
new to me,
lives in the soul,

first you've got to be true to your-self, oh yeah.
such a ver-y re-cent turn of e-vents.
like a mel-o-dy that I can't for-get, oh no.

It don't mat-ter 'bout no-bod - y else, oh
And the truth does-n't make an - y sense, oh
It's a mem-o - ry with just one re-gret, oh

no, if it's there in your mind.
no, for the ver - y first time.
yeah: just a lit - tle more time.

It's a les - son I've just come to
It's a les - son that I had to
If we had an - oth - er year or

21

C | F | G

say - ing it's al - right to show_
say - ing it's time_ to be grow -
say - ing it's al - right to show_

F | C

To Coda ⊕

_ your face_ to the world.
- ing old - er, my friend. _
_ your face_ now.

1.

2.

D.S. al Coda

Ev-'ry-thing seems

You're a mem-o - ry that

CODA
⊕ C | F | C

If you want to be true to me,

F | C

first you've got to be true to your-self, oh yeah.

F | C

It don't mat-ter 'bout no - bod - y else, oh

F | C | G | C/G

no. Keep me there in your mind. _

G7 | C | F/C | C

I'll be there by your side.

BACK IN L.A.

Words and Music by
NEIL DIAMOND

BE
from JONATHAN LIVINGSTON SEAGULL,
the film by Hall Bartlett

Words and Music by
NEIL DIAMOND

Lost on a paint-ed sky, __ where the clouds are hung __ for the po-et's eye, __ you may find __ him, if you may find him.

There on a dis-tant shore __ by the wings of dreams __ through an o-pen door, __ you may know __ him, if you may..

Be   as a page that aches_ for a

word which speaks_ on a   theme that is time - less__

while the sun god will make for your

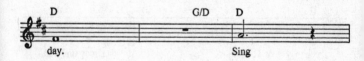

day.   Sing

as a song in search_ of a   voice that is si - lent,__

and the   one   God   will

make   for __ your   way.

BEAUTIFUL NOISE

Words and Music by
NEIL DIAMOND

It's the song of the kids, ___

and it plays ___ un - til dark. ___

It's the song of the

cars on their fu - ri - ous flights. ___
Noise made of joy and of strife. ___

But there's e - ven ro - mance ___
Like a sym - pho - ny played ___

___ in the way ___ that they dance ___ to the beat ___ of the lights. ___
___ by the pass - ing pa - rade, ___ it's the mu - sic of life. ___

It's a Beau - ti - ful Noise,

and it's a sound that I love.

And it fits me as well _____
And it makes me feel good, _____

as a hand in a glove.
like a hand in a glove.

Yes it does; _____

_____ yes it does. _____

What a Beau - ti - ful Noise

com - in' in - to my room. _____

And it's beg - gin' for me

just to give it a tune.

BLUE DESTINY

Words and Music by
NEIL DIAMOND

Moderately

C

Once you were mine,_ and you want-ed the whole world to know._
First, you de - cide _ that our love will al - ways be true._

G/C   C   G/C C Em7/B Am

Now ev-'ry time I'm a - round,_
Next thing I know,   you're run -

you've got some-where to go. _
ning with some - bod - y   new. _

G

I ask my heart ev-'ry day, _
Once you were just mine a - lone. _

F   C

"Can there be some oth - er   way?" _ }
Now you're just some-one I've known. _ }

Tell me,

33

THE BEST YEARS OF OUR LIVES

Words and Music by
NEIL DIAMOND

Brightly

Hey lis - ten to the work-ing man.

Can you hear the dream ___ that re - sides ___ in his soul?

___ And when you hear that poor man sing-in',

can you hear a sto - ry that cries ___ to be told? ___

___ Wan-na hear you say 'oh yeah.' ___

I need to hear you say 'oh yeah.'

36

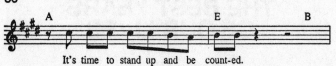
It's time to stand up and be count-ed.

These are the days of our be - gin-nings.

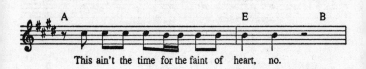
This ain't the time for the faint of heart, no.

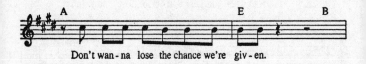
Don't wan-na lose the chance we're giv-en.

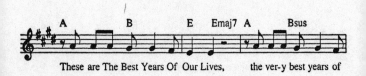
These are The Best Years Of Our Lives, the ver-y best years of

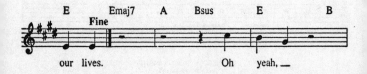
our lives.   Oh   yeah, __

hear the song of wom-an-kind. Car-ried 'til she

ached; now she's tak-in' her stand. ___ Says she's got the

right to be right be-side and e-qual with ev - 'ry man. ___

Wan-na hear you say 'oh ___ yeah.'

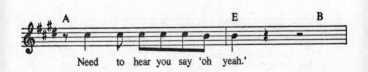

Need to hear you say 'oh yeah.'

D.S. al Fine

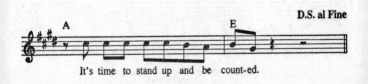

It's time to stand up and be count-ed.

BLUE HIGHWAY

Words and Music by
NEIL DIAMOND and HARLAN HOWARD

So long, big cit-y; it's
So long con-fu-sion; it's

time to say good-bye. I'm long-ing for those
time to slow things down. Say good-bye to

coun-try roads; I need to see the sky.
my old friends, ease on out of town.

Think I'll take a swing down south,
I made me some mon-ey here

vis-it Ten-nes-see. See if that girl
but paid for ev-'ry day. And ev-'ry mile just

An-nie still re-mem-bers me.
makes me smile, 'cause I made my get-a-way.

THE BOAT THAT I ROW

Words and Music by
NEIL DIAMOND

Moderately, in a Gospel style

I don't have a lot, ___ but with me that's fine. ___
There ain't a man a-live ___ can tell me what to say. ___

What-ev - er I got,
I choose my own side, ___

___ well, I know ___ it's mine. ___
___ and I like ___ it that way. ___

I don't go a - round
I don't wor - ry a - bout ___

___ with the lo - cal crowd. ___
___ all the things ___ that I'm not. ___

I don't dig what's in, ___
There's on - ly one thing ___

so I guess_ I'm out.____
that I want_ I ain't got.____

I'm say-in' these things_ so you know_ me, ba-
You know that I'm talk-in' a-bout_ you, ba-

- by,
- by.

so you un-der-stand_
But you bet-ter know_

_ what I'm all_ a-bout.
_ be-fore you come a-long.

The Boat That I

Row won't cross no o - cean; The Boat That I

Row won't get_ me there soon._

But I got the love_

_ and if you_ got the no - tion, The Boat That I

D.S. and Fade
(2nd time)

Row's big e-nough for two, just me and you.

BROOKLYN ON A SATURDAY NIGHT

Words and Music by
NEIL DIAMOND

When they met,_ it was right._
oh, he tried_ to do right._   But

Fell right in_ with the beat_   in
things got mis - un-der-stood_   in

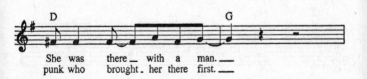

Brook-lyn On A Sat-ur-day Night.
Brook-lyn On A Sat-ur-day Night.   He

He had_ noth-ing much planned.
end-ed up hav-ing some words   with the

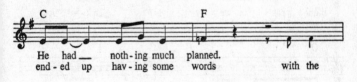

She was there_ with a man._
punk who brought_ her there first._

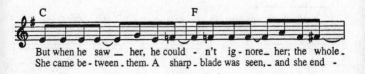

But when he saw _ her, he could - n't ig - nore_ her; the whole_
She came be - tween _ them. A sharp_ blade was seen,_ and she end -

44

CANTA LIBRE

Words and Music by
NEIL DIAMOND

ños, Can-ta Li - bre.

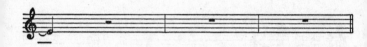

I got mu - sic run-nin' in my head,
I got mu - sic run-nin' in my brain,

makes me feel
ev - 'ry song

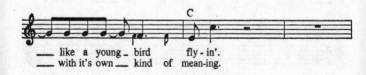

like a young bird fly - in'.
with it's own kind of mean-ing.

'Cross my mind and lay - in' in my bed,
Cleanse the soul and wash a - way the pain,

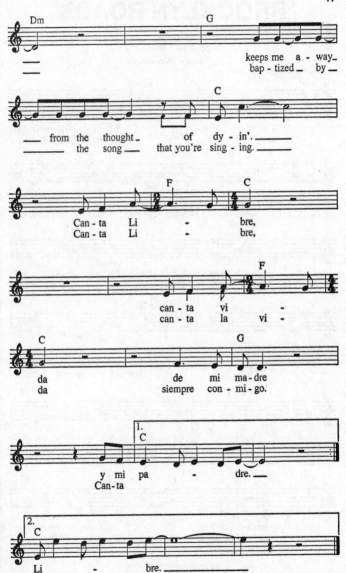

BROOKLYN ROADS

Words and Music by
NEIL DIAMOND

BROTHER LOVE'S TRAVELING SALVATION SHOW

Words and Music by
NEIL DIAMOND

- ged tent ___ where there _ ain't _ no trees, ___
- ___ and slow ___ like a ____ small _ earth - quake,.

and that gos - pel group ___ tell-in' you ___
and when he ___ lets go, ___ half the val-

- ley shakes._ } It's Love, Broth-er Love, say, Broth-

- er Love's Trav-el-ing Sal - va-tion Show. _ (Hal-

- le... hal - le...) Pack up the ba - bies and grab_

- ___ the old la - dies and ev - 'ry-one goes,_ cause

ev-'ry-one knows _ Broth-er Love's show. (Instrumental)

Broth-er Love's show. (Hal-le-lu - jah!) *(Spoken:) Brothers!*

(Hal-le... hal - le - lu - jah!) (Hal-le - lu - *I said, brothers!*

- jah!) (Hal-le... hal - le - lu - jah!) *Now you've got yourself two good hands. And when your brother is troubled,*

(Hal-le - lu - jah!) (Hal-le... hal- *you gotta reach out your one hand for him, 'cause that's what it's there for.*

- le - lu - jah!) (Hal-le - lu - jah!) *And when you heart is troubled, you gotta*

(Hal-le...hal - le - lu - jah!) (Hal-le - lu - *reach out your other hand, reach it out to the man up there, 'cause that's what He's there for.*

- jah!) (Hal-le... hal - le - lu - jah!)

Hymn-like

Take my hand ___ in yours, ___ walk with me ___

___ this day. ___ In my heart ___ I know.

I will nev - er stray. ___

Hal-le... hal - le... hal - le... hal - le... hal-

D.S. al Coda

- le... hal - le... hal - le... hal - le...

CODA

Broth- er Love's show. ____ A - men.

CAN ANYBODY HEAR ME

Words and Music by NEIL DIAMOND
and BILL LaBOUNTY

CAPTAIN SUNSHINE

Words and Music by
NEIL DIAMOND

CRACKLIN' ROSIE

Words and Music by
NEIL DIAMOND

Moderately fast

Crack-lin' Ros-ie, get on board.

We're gon-na ride till there ain't no more to

go, tak-in' it slow. And Lord don't you

know I'll have me a time with a poor man's la - dy!

1. Hitch-in' on a twi-light train;
2.,(D.S.) Crack-lin' Ros-ie make me smile, and

ain't noth-ing here that I care to take a-
girl if it lasts for an hour, that's all

long,   may - be   a   song ___
right.   We got   all   night ___

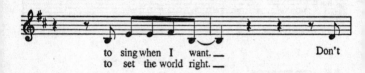

to sing when I   want. ___   Don't
to set the world right. ___

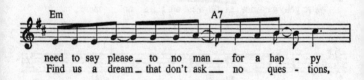

need to say please ___ to no man ___ for a hap - py
Find us a dream ___ that don't ask ___ no   ques - tions,

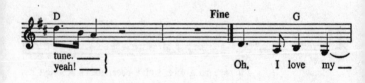

tune. ___ }   Oh,   I love my ___
yeah! ___

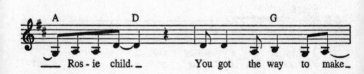

___ Ros - ie child. ___   You got the way to make ___

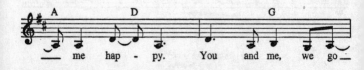

___ me hap - py.   You   and me, we go ___

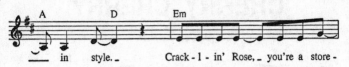

__ in style. _ Crack-1-in' Rose, _ you're a store-

-bought wom-an, but you make me feel _ like a gui-

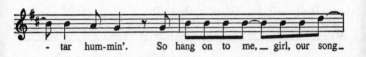

-tar hum-min'. So hang on to me, _ girl, our song _

_ keeps run-nin' on. _____

Play it now! _ Play it now! _

1. Play it now, _ my ba-by! 2. Play it now, _ my ba-by! D.S. al Fine

CHERRY, CHERRY

Words and Music by
NEIL DIAMOND

61

CRUNCHY GRANOLA SUITE

Words and Music by
NEIL DIAMOND

_ deet   deet _ deet   dee - dle dee doo. _

N.C.   A   G/A

{ Though it don't _
{ And like a

A   E7/A   A

_ say   much _ and it won't _ of - fend, _ if you sing
man with a ti - ger out - side _ his gate, _ he

D/A

_ it at school, _ they're lia - ble to send _ you home _
not on - ly could - n't re - lax, _ but he could - n't re - late. _

A   G/A

_   nev - er know - in'   what you're
_   Now he can. _   Fam - 'ly

___ 3 ___   Delete this bar 2nd time

show - in';   think you're grow - in'   your own
man; _   tried my

tea. _____   (Dig!)
brand. _____

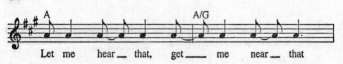

Let me hear_ that, get_ me near_ that

Crunch-y Gran-o-la Suite. _

Drop your shrink,_ and stop_ your drink - in';

crunch-y gran-o-la's neat! _

Sing it out! _   All

right!   (Spoken:) I'll have a double, please.

DESIRÉE

Words and Music by
NEIL DIAMOND

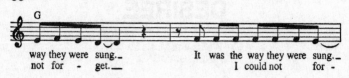

way they were sung.___ It was the way they were sung.___
not for - get.___ I could not for -

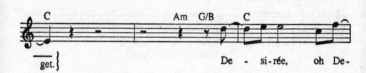

___ get.⎬ De - si - rée, oh De -

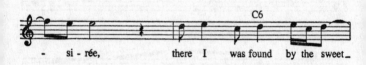

- si - rée, there I was found by the sweet___

___ pas - sion sound of your lov - ing song.

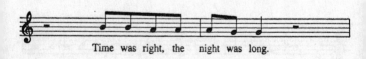

Time was right, the night was long.

Re-mem-ber, De - si - rée, oh De - si - rée?

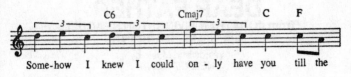

Some-how I knew I could on - ly have you till the

morn-ing light.
{ If on - ly for that
{ The night was long, the

sin - gle night,
time was right.

sweet De-si-rée, you

made it right.

Then came the

Do you re - mem-ber, De -

Repeat and Fade

- si - rée,   oh De   -   si - rée?

DEAR FATHER
from JONATHAN LIVINGSTON SEAGULL, the film by Hall Bartlett

Words and Music by
NEIL DIAMOND

69

DO IT

Words and Music by
NEIL DIAMOND

DONE TOO SOON

Words and Music by
NEIL DIAMOND

Moderately

Je-sus Christ, Fan - ny Brice, Wolf - ie Mo - zart and

Hum - phrey Bo - gart and Gen - ghis Khan and on

to H. G. Wells.

Ho Chi Minh, Gun - ga Din, Hen - ry Luce and John

Wilkes Booth and Al - ex - an - ders King and Gra-ham Bell.

Ra - mar Krish - na, Ma -

- ma Whist-ler, Pat-rice Lu-mum-ba and Russ _ Co-lum-bo,

Karl and Chi - co Marx, _ Al - bert _ Ca - mus. _

E. A. Poe, Hen-ri _____ Rous-seau, Sho -

- lom A-leich - em and Car - yl Chess-man, Al -

- an Freed _ and Bus - ter Kea - ton, too. _

And each one there has one thing shared: _ They have

A tempo

sweat-ed be-neath the same ___ sun,

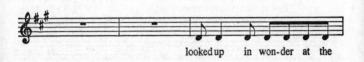

looked up in won-der at the

same moon, and

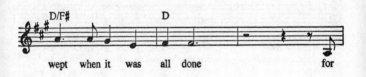

wept when it was all done for

be-in' Done Too _ Soon... for

be-in' Done _ Too Soon. ____

EVERYBODY

Words and Music by
NEIL DIAMOND and JESSE DIAMOND

In a relaxed two

Ev-'ry-bod-y needs some-one that they're gon-na be-
Ev-'ry-bod-y needs some-one, but it's got-ta mean
And I'm glad I have you there, 'cause I would-'ve been

lieve in. Ev-'ry-bod-y's the same a-
some-thing. Giv-ing up a piece of you's the
no-where. Be-in' here all a-lone's a

round the world. If you wan-na find
hard-est part. If you wan-na have
lone-ly sound. Ev-'ry-bod-y needs

some-one, then you on-ly have to show it.
some-one, then you real-ly got to know it.
some-one that they're gon-na be-lieve in.

Noth-in's sad-der than love that's left un-heard.
Does-n't take ver-y much to break a heart.
Ev-'ry-bod-y's the same a-round the world.

Me, how I tried to__ de-ny__ that it
May_ I get lost in__ your eyes__ for a

point-ed to you.
life-time__ or two?

FIRE ON THE TRACKS

Words and Music by
NEIL DIAMOND

FOREVER IN BLUE JEANS

Words and Music by
NEIL DIAMOND and RICHARD BENNETT

Moderately

Mon-ey talks.__ But it don't sing and dance,__ and it don't walk.__ And long as I __ can have you here with me,__ I'd much rath-er be.__ For-ev-er In Blue Jeans. Hon-ey's sweet. But it ain't noth-ing next to ba-by's treat.__ And if you par-don me,__ I'd like to say__ we'll

do o - kay___ For-ev-er In Blue Jeans.

May-be to - night.___ May-be to - night, ___

___ you and I ___ all a - lone ___ by the fire; ___

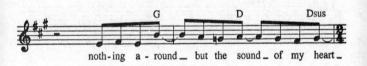

noth-ing a - round ___ but the sound ___ of my heart ___

___ and your sighs. ___

Mon-ey talks. ___ But it can't sing and dance, ___ and

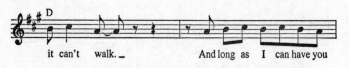

it can't walk. _ And long as I can have you

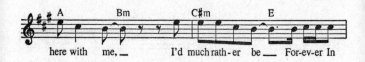

here with me, _ I'd much rath-er be _ For-ev-er In

Blue Jeans, babe. _ Hon-ey's sweet. _

But it ain't noth-ing next to ba-by's treat. _

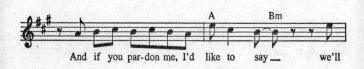

And if you par-don me, I'd like to say _ we'll

do o - kay _ For-ev-er In Blue Jeans.

THE GIFT OF SONG

Words and Music by
NEIL DIAMOND

GIRL, YOU'LL BE
A WOMAN SOON

Words and Music by
NEIL DIAMOND

84

"The boy's no good." — Well, I

fi - nal - ly found what I've been look-ing for, — but if

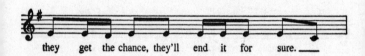
they get the chance, they'll end it for sure. —

Sure they would. — Ba - by, I've

done all I could. It's up to you,

CODA

man. Soon

you'll need a man. —

GITCHY GOOMY

Words and Music by
NEIL DIAMOND

Gitch-y Goom-y, gitch-y gad-dy,
Gitch-y Goom-y, gitch-y gad-dy,

sit you lad-die down on your dad-dy's knee.
sit you lad-die down while I have my say.

And ain't it a
Now don't be

nice place to be?
run-nin' a - way.

Gog-gin nog-gin, pa-pa's rock-in'
Gog-gin nog-gin, pa-pa's talk-in'.

like a mock-in'-bird in a wind-y tree.
Don't be walk - in' off like you mean to play.

86

And that ain't no ___
Well, you can have ___

___ place for me.
___ it your way.

Been there one time; been there two ___ times.
Been there one time; been there two ___ times.

Been there three ___ times more ___ than I care ___ to be. ___
Been there three ___ times more ___ than I care ___ to say. ___

But
But

we're gon - na make ___ it through, ___ Gitch - y Goom -
you're gon - na be ___ o - kay, ___ Gitch - y Goom -

Fine

- y. }
- y. }

Life is good, ___

GLORY ROAD

Words and Music by
NEIL DIAMOND

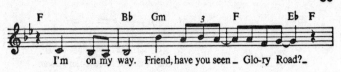

I'm on my way. Friend, have you seen _ Glo-ry Road?_

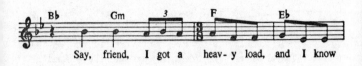

Say, friend, I got a heav-y load, and I know

glo - ry road's wait-ing for me.

me. Ba ba ba ba ba da da da da da da da

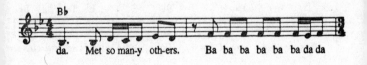

da. Met so man-y oth-ers. Ba ba ba ba ba ba da da

da da da da da da. Want-ed to know_ which way to go. _

_ Lou'-si - an-a, _____ New _ York

Cit - y. _____ They want-ed the an - swer.

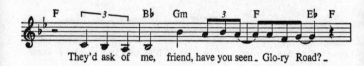

They'd ask of me, friend, have you seen Glo-ry Road? _

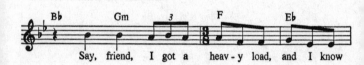

Say, friend, I got a heav-y load, and I know

glo - ry road's wait - ing for me.

Rest my load, now I know Glo-ry Road won't set me free. _

_ Ba ba ba ba ba da da da da da da da

da. Ba ba ba ba ba da da da da da da da da.

GUITAR HEAVEN

Words and Music by
NEIL DIAMOND

Moderately

Hey lit-tle boy just sit-tin' on your back porch

pick-in' on your gui-tar wish-ing you were far a - way.

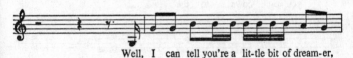

Well, I can tell you're a lit-tle bit of dream-er,

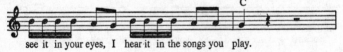

see it in your eyes, I hear it in the songs you play.

And hey lit-tle boy, just play it like you feel it.

Make it so real it's al - most too real to take.

Just swing it like a play-er, make it like a prayer. It's

one from the heart, give it all of the heart it can take.

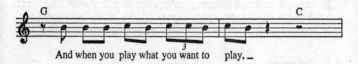

And when you play what you want to play, __

you reach down __ to the soul. __

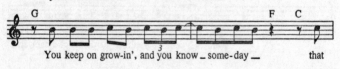

You keep on grow-in', and you know __ some-day __ that

sound is gon-na turn in-to gold. __ Boy, you're tak-in' me there, __

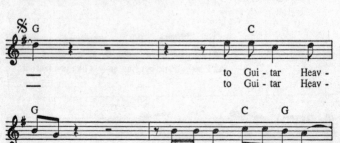

to Gui-tar Heav-
to Gui-tar Heav-

en. __ And with-out say-in' a word, __
en. __ You make me feel ev-'ry sound; __

GOLD DON'T RUST

Words and Music by NEIL DIAMOND,
GARY BURR and BOB DiPIERO

I know you wor - ry ev - 'ry time_ I_
wish that I_ could give_ you what_ you_

go_ a - way._ You won - der will_ these
need_ from me._ But what good is_ a

sweet, sweet feel - ings_ shine_ or fade._ Well,
prom - ise or a_ guar - an - tee?_

that's a ques - tion you don't have_ to ask.
Love is still_ a sim - ple act_ of faith.

What heav - en makes,_ it al - ways makes to last.
And a faith - ful heart_ is al - ways worth the wait._

Gold Don't Rust._

HEADED FOR THE FUTURE

Words by NEIL DIAMOND
Music by NEIL DIAMOND,
TOM HENSLEY and ALAN LINDGREN

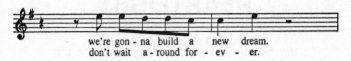

we're gon - na build a new dream.
don't wait a - round for - ev - er.

We've got to make it stand tall.
We've got to do it right now.

It's got to last a long time. }
Let's do it all to - geth - er. }

C   D♭   D   E♭   B♭   F

Lean on me, ___   and

E♭   B♭   F

I'm gon - na lean on ___ you. ___   We're

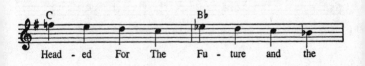

C   B♭

Head - ed   For   The   Fu - ture   and   the

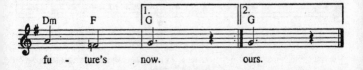

Dm   F   1.   2.
                         G   G

fu - ture's   now.   ours.

HEARTLIGHT

Words and Music by NEIL DIAMOND,
BURT BACHARACH and CAROLE BAYER SAGER

Heart-light in the mid-dle of a young boy's dream.

Don't wake me up too soon.

Gon-na take a ride a-cross the moon,

you and me.

He's look-in' for

CODA

you and me.

Turn on your Heart - light now.

Turn on your Heart - light now.

HOLLY HOLY

Words and Music by
NEIL DIAMOND

102

And the seed,_ let it be_ filled with to - mor - row,

Hol-ly Ho - ly._

D.S. al Coda

CODA

Hol - ly Ho - ly dream,_

dream of on - ly you._

Hol - hol-ly ho - ho-ly sun;_

Hol. - Hol-ly Ho - ly rain._

Hol - ly Ho - ly love.

HELLO AGAIN
from the Motion Picture THE JAZZ SINGER

Words by NEIL DIAMOND
Music by NEIL DIAMOND and ALAN LINDGREN

HOOKED ON THE MEMORY OF YOU

Words and Music by
NEIL DIAMOND

Moderately

E

Stay with me, here with me. Long as you're

A

near with me, I'm your man,

F#m7   **B7**   **%**   **E**

Hooked On The Mem-'ry Of You and I.
love with me,

Who knows why? I on-ly know that I'm
lie with me. Spend your de-sire with me.

A   **F#m7**

sure I am
I'm your man,

Hooked On The

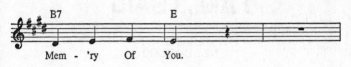

Mem - 'ry Of You.

Time, time stand - ing still,

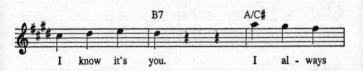

I know it's you. I al - ways

will need you to

CODA

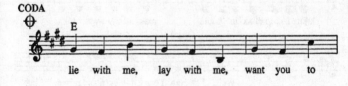

lie with me, lay with me, want you to

stay with me. Know I am

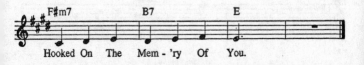

Hooked On The Mem - 'ry Of You.

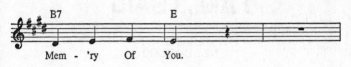 107

I AM...I SAID

Words and Music by
NEIL DIAMOND

L. A.'s fine, the sun shines most the time

and the feel-in' is lay back.

Palm trees grow, and rents are low. But you

know I keep think-in' 'bout mak-in' my way back.

Well, I'm New York Cit-y born and raised, but

now-a-days, I'm lost be-tween two shores.

L. A.'s fine, but it ain't home.

be-in' a king _ and then be-came one ? _

Well, ex-cept for the names _ and a few oth-er chang - es, if you

talk a-bout me, _ the sto - ry's the same one.

But I got an emp-ti-ness deep in - side. _

And I've tried, _ but it won't let me go. And

I'm not a man who likes _ to swear, but

I've nev - er cared for the sound of be - in' a -

D.S. al Fine

lone. _____ "I Am," I

I'VE BEEN THIS WAY BEFORE

Words and Music by
NEIL DIAMOND

I've seen the light, and I've seen the flame. And I've Been This Way Be-fore and I'm sure to be this way a - gain. For I've been re - fused, and I've been re - gained. And I've seen your eyes be - fore, and I'm sure to see your eyes a - gain, once a - gain. For

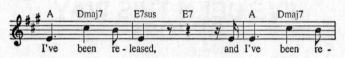

I've been re - leased,　　　and I've been re -

gained.　　　And I've sung　my song be - fore, and I'm

sure to sing my song a - gain,　　once a-gain.

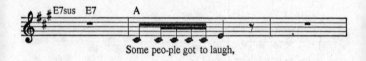

Some peo-ple got to laugh,

some peo-ple got to cry,　　　some peo-ple　　got to

make it through　　by nev - er won-d'ring why.

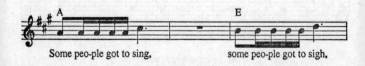

Some peo-ple got to sing,　　　some peo-ple got to sigh,

some peo-ple nev-er see the light un -

til the day they die. _____ But I've been re -

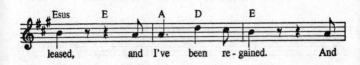

leased, and I've been re - gained. And

I've Been This Way Be-fore, and I'm sure to be this way a -

gain, once a - gain. One more time a -

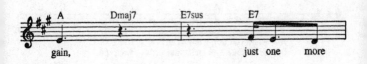

gain, just one more

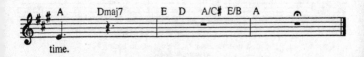

time.

I GOT THE FEELIN'
(Oh No, No)

Words and Music by
NEIL DIAMOND

Slowly, with feeling

Oh no, no,___ no, no,___ ba - by, some-thing's wrong.___
Oh no, no,___ no, no,___ you don't smile the same. ___

Oh no, no,___ no, no,___
Oh no, no,___ no, no,___

___ that old-time fire is gone. ___
___ like you been hid - in' pain. ___

It's not so much the things you say, love.
I love you so much I could taste it,

It's what you don't say I'm a - fraid of.
but girl, your eyes tell me it's wast-ed.

I Got The Feel - in' I'm

hear-in' good-bye. ___ Don't have to say ___ it; it's

there in your eyes. ___ Oh why,

1. oh my. 2. oh my.

Oh no, oh no,

no, oh no, ___ ba-by,

I Got The Feel - in' I'm hear-in' good-bye; ___

Repeat and Fade

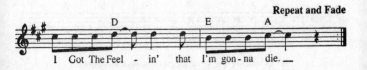

I Got The Feel - in' that I'm gon-na die. ___

I'M A BELIEVER

Words and Music by
NEIL DIAMOND

I'M ALIVE

Words and Music by
NEIL DIAMOND and DAVID FOSTER

Take a walk, you can hard - ly breathe the air.
Ev - 'ry night on the streets of Hol - ly-wood,
(Instrumental)

Look a-round, it's a hard life ev - 'ry-where.
pret - ty girls want to give you some - thing good.

Peo - ple talk, but they nev - er real - ly care.
Love for sale, it's a lone - ly town at night,

On the street there's a feel - ing of de-spair. But
ther - a - py for a heart mis - un - der-stood. But
(Sung:) And

ev - 'ry-day there's a brand new ba - by born, and
look a-round; there's a flower on ev - 'ry street.
ev - 'ry-day there's a brand new ba - by born, and

ev - 'ry-day there's the sun to keep you warm, and
Look a-round, well, it's grow - ing at your feet. And
ev - 'ry way there's e - nough to keep you warm, and

it's al - right. ___   Yeah, it's al - right. ___
ev - 'ry - day ___   you can hear me say: ___
it's o - kay. ___   Hey I'm glad to say: ___

Chorus

I'm A - live. _____   And I don't. ___
I'm A - live. _____   I wan - na
I'm A - live. _____   And I don't. ___

___ care much. for words ___ of doom. ___ If it's
take all that life has got ___ to give. ___ All I
___ care much. for words ___ of doom. ___ If it's

love you need, ___ I've got ___ the room. ___ It's a sim-
need is some - one to share ___ it with. ___ I've got love
love you need, ___ I've got ___ the room. ___ It's a sim-

- ple thing ___ that came ___ to me ___ and I
___ and love ___ is all ___ I real - ly need. ___
- ple thing ___ that came ___ to me ___ when I ___

___ thank God: ___ I'm A - live. _____
___ to live: ___ I'm A - live. _____
___ found you: ___ I'm A - live. _____

Last time repeat Chorus, ad lib. and Fade

I'm A - live. _____
I'm A - live. _____
I'm A - live. _____

IF I LOST MY WAY

Words and Music by NEIL DIAMOND
and GARY BURR

In a flowing manner

If I Lost My Way, would you stand with me, would you love me still and care for what I need If I Lost My Way?

If I lost the faith to face up to the test, would I let you down?

could I keep your trust? Promise that our love

Would you love me less
would not turn to dust

IF THERE WERE NO DREAMS

Words and Music by
NEIL DIAMOND and MICHEL LEGRAND

IF YOU KNOW
WHAT I MEAN

Words and Music by
NEIL DIAMOND

And the ra-di-o played like a car-ni-val tune as we lay in our bed in the oth-er room, when we gave it a-way for the sake of a dream in a pen-ny ar-cade, If You Know What I Mean. Here's to the songs we used to sing, and here's to the times we used to know. It's hard to hold them in our arms a-gain but hard to let them go. Do you

IN MY LIFETIME

Words and Music by
NEIL DIAMOND

Moderately

Hey boy, you got the ad-dress on the street of un-knowns. Big man smok-in' on a ci-gar, deal-in' on the tel-e-phone. Hey boy, look out for flim-flam if you wan-na go real far. Been there, and I be-lieve you got to be what you are. In My

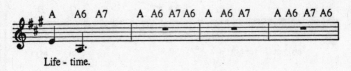

Life - time.

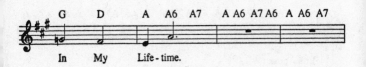

In My Life - time.

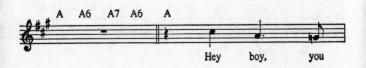

Hey boy, you

look like a mil-lion. Hey now,

show 'em what you got. Hey boy,

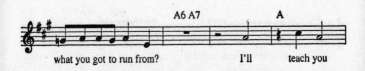

what you got to run from? I'll teach you

all that I for-got.　　　　In　My

Life - time.

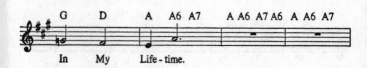

In　My　Life - time.

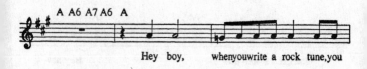

Hey boy,　　when you write a rock tune, you

give up　a piece of your　soul. _　　Stay boy

un - der-neath a rock-in' moon;　try be-fore you get too　old. _

Hoo - ray,   got your-self a road gig;

an - y gig's gon-na be   fine. _   O - kay, you

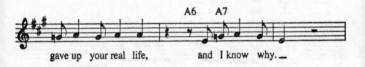

gave up your real life,   and I know why. _

In My Life - time,   I   have

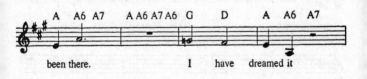

been there.   I   have   dreamed it

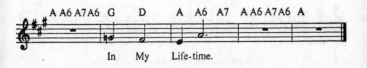

In   My   Life-time.

KENTUCKY WOMAN

Words and Music by
NEIL DIAMOND

Moderately fast

Ken-tuck-y Wom-an, she shines with her own
Well, she ain't the kind makes heads turn at the drop

kind of light.
of her name.

She'd look at you once, and a day that's all wrong
But some-thing in - side that she's got turns you on

looks all right.
just the same.
And I love
And she loves

her; God know, I love her.
me; God knows, she loves me.

Ken-tuck-y Wom - an, if she get to

know you, she goin' to own you,

LADY-OH

Words and Music by
NEIL DIAMOND

La-dy-oh, La-dy-oh, I walked the streets a-gain last night. I saw you in the cit-y light like a vi-sion, La-dy-oh. La-dy I, La-dy I, I've been wait-in' a-round such a long long time be-liev-in' I could make you mine,

LET ME TAKE YOU IN MY ARMS AGAIN

Words and Music by
NEIL DIAMOND

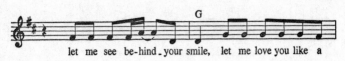

let me see be-hind your smile, let me love you like a

child, let me take you in my arms.

I'm like a train that's roll - in' on a track,

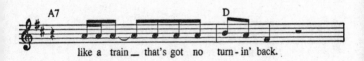

like a train that's got no turn-in' back.

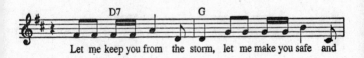

Let me keep you from the storm, let me make you safe and

warm, let me take you in my arms.

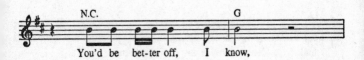

You'd be bet-ter off, I know,

with an-oth-er kind of man.

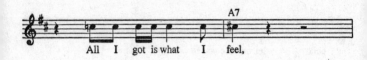

All I got is what I feel,

and what I feel is what I am.

Let Me Take You In My Arms A-gain.

Won't be eas-y, but I'll learn to bend.

Like a ship with-out a sail on a sea with-out a

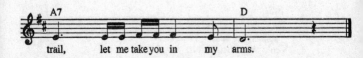

trail, let me take you in my arms.

LONELY LOOKING SKY

Words and Music by
NEIL DIAMOND

never made it right, never made it right,

lone-ly look-ing night, lone-ly look-ing night,

lone-ly look-ing night. _____

(Instrumental) Sleep, _____

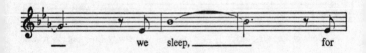

_____ we sleep, _____ for

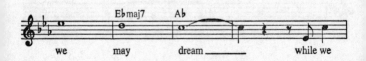

we may dream _____ while we

may. Dream _____ we

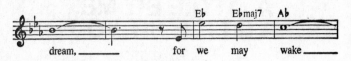

dream, _____ for we may wake _____

_____ one more day, _____ one more day.

Glo-ry look-ing day, glo-ry day, glo-ry look-ing day,

and all its glo-ry told a sim-ple way. Be -

hold it if you may, glo-ry look-ing day,

glo-ry look-ing day,

Lone-ly Look-ing Sky. _____

A LITTLE BIT ME,
A LITTLE BIT YOU

Words and Music by
NEIL DIAMOND

you know that it's true. ___

It's a lit-tle bit me. ___

It's a lit-tle bit you."

Don't know just what I said wrong, but

girl, I a-pol-o-gize. ___

Don't go, here's where you feel love, so

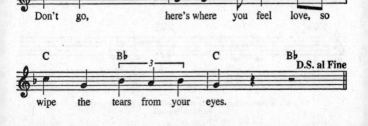

wipe the tears from your eyes.

MARRY ME

Words and Music by NEIL DIAMOND
and TOM SHAPIRO

Gently

Say that you'll Mar - ry Me,
Prom - ise you'll stay ___ with me.

some - times car - ry me.
We'll make some mem - o - ries,

And I will be there ___ for - ev - er - more.
and may - be a dream ___ or two ___ will come.

___ true.
for you. ___
Who knows? ___

And if you Mar - ry Me,
This I can say ___ for sure:

I will give ev - 'ry - thing.
all that I have is yours.

And I will do an - y - thing _ that you need _
You'll nev - er won - der where _ I stand; _

me to. ____ }
it shows. _ }

You'll know _ by the love _

_ in my eyes _ and the beat of my heart, _ I'll be there. _

_ You'll know, _ 'cause you'll nev -

- er be lone - ly a - gain, _ an - y-time, an - y - where. _

To Coda

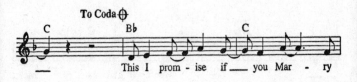

_ This I prom - ise if _ you Mar - ry

D.C. al Coda

Me.

CODA

All I prom - ise you ___ I will ___ be

if you'll on - ly say ___ you'll Mar - ry Me. ___

___ I won't ev - er for - get ___ these words, ___

___ and I'll love you for all ___ I'm worth ___

___ if you say you will Mar - ry Me. ___

___ Won't you Mar - ry Me? ___

___ Mar - ry Me.

LONGFELLOW SERENADE

Words and Music by
NEIL DIAMOND

Long - fel - low Se - re - nade, ___
Long - fel - low Se - re - nade, ___

such were the plans ___ I'd made. ___ For
such were the plans ___ I made. ___ But

she was a la - dy, and I was a dream-er
she was a la - dy as deep as the riv - er,

with on - ly words to trade. ___ You know that I was
and through the night we stayed. ___ And in my way, I

born for a night like this, ___
loved her as none be - fore, ___

warmed by a sto - len kiss. ___ For I was
loved her with words and more. ___ For she was

E … **B7**

lone-ly,   and she was lone-ly. ——
lone-ly,   and I was lone-ly. ——

E

Ride, —— come on ba - by, ride. —

Emaj7   **E7**   **A**

Let me make your dreams —

E   **B7**

come   true.   I'll sing — my

E   **Emaj7**

song; —— let me sing my song. ——

E7   **A**   **E**

— Let me make it warm   for

B7   **E**

you.   I'll weave his web — of rhyme

up - on the sum - mer night. ___

We'll leave this world - ly time

on his wing - ed flight. ___

Then come, and as ___ we lay

be - side this sleep - y glade, ___

there I ___ will sing ___ to you ___ my

Long - fel - low Se - re - nade. *(Instrumental)*

LOVE ON THE ROCKS
from the Motion Picture THE JAZZ SINGER

Words and Music by
NEIL DIAMOND and GILBERT BECAUD

Moderately slow ballad

Love On The Rocks ain't no sur-prise.

Pour me a drink, __ and I'll tell you some lies. __

Got noth-in' to lose, __ so you just sing the blues all the

time. Gave you my heart,

gave you my soul. You left me a-lone __ here __ with

noth-ing to hold. __ Yes-ter-day's gone.

Now all I want is a smile.

First they say _ they want _ you,

how they real-ly need _ you. Sud-den-ly, you find _ you're out _ there,

walk-ing in a storm. When they know _ they have _ you,

then they _ real-ly have you. _ Noth-ing you _ can do _ or say. _ you've

got to leave, _ just get a-way. We all _ know the song.

You need what you need, you can say what you want. _

Not much you can do when the feel-ing is gone. May be

blue skies a-bove, but it's cold when your love's on the

rocks. *(Instrumental)*

A MATTER OF LOVE

Words and Music by NEIL DIAMOND
and TOM SHAPIRO

With a strong backbeat

If you've been feel - in' blue, __
We got mag - ic here; __

hey, it's been __ the same for me. __
it's the pow - er of love, I know. __

Now I'm here
It's danc - in' in

with you, __ and you're ex - act -
the air, and I can feel

- ly what I need.
the feel - in' grow. __

Put your de - fens - es down. __ Let me show __
Put your de - fens - es down. __ Let me hold __

154

don't you know it's A Mat-ter Of Love.

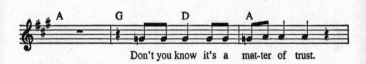

Don't you know it's a mat-ter of trust.

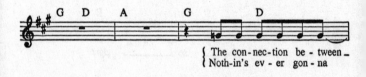

{ The con-nec-tion be - tween _
{ Noth-in's ev - er gon - na

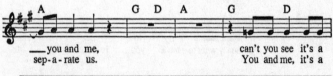

_ you and me,   can't you see it's a
sep-a-rate us.   You and me, it's a

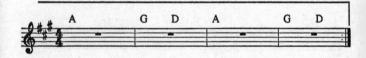

1.

mat-ter of trust, mat-ter of us, mat-ter of love.

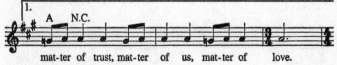

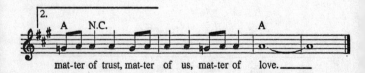

2.

mat-ter of trust, mat-ter of us, mat-ter of love.____

A MODERN DAY VERSION OF LOVE

Words and Music by
NEIL DIAMOND

com - fort of ____ A

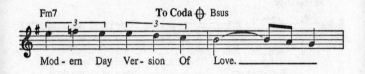

Mod - ern Day Ver - sion Of Love. ____

(Instrumental)

Close my eyes and keep on run - ning, re - a - lize it

is - n't gon - na work an - y - more ___

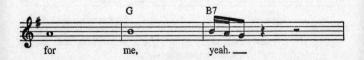

for me, yeah. ___

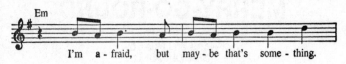

Em
I'm a-fraid, but may-be that's some-thing.

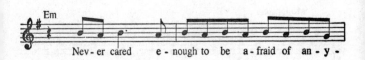

Em
Nev-er cared e-nough to be a-fraid of an-y-

Am **D** **G**
thing be - fore, _____

B7   **D.C. al Coda**
not be - fore. _____

CODA

B   **Em9**
Love. _____

Em

MERRY-GO-ROUND

Words and Music by
NEIL DIAMOND

The rich and the poor, ___

the rich get a maid,. and she takes ___
seems like there ain't ___ much dif -

___ all the kids ___ to the zoo. ___
- f'rence be - tween ___ the two. ___

It's true.   The
It's true.   The

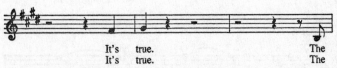

poor got no maid,. so they pack ___ up their kids ___ and go
bad cheat some-one ___ and get caught. while the good ___ nev - er do. .

MORNINGSIDE

Words and Music by
NEIL DIAMOND

Morn-ing - side, _ the
Morn-ing - light, _
Morn-ing - side, _ an

old man died, and
morn-ing bright, I
old man died, and

no one cried. They
spent the night with
no one cried. He

sim - ply turned _ a - way. And when he died,
dreams that make _ you weep. Morn-ing time, _
sure - ly died _ a - lone. And truth is sad, _

he left a ta - ble made of
wash a - way the sad - ness from these
for not a child _ would claim the

nails and pride, and _ with his hands
eyes of mine, for I re - call _
gift he had. The words he carved.

he carved these words in - side:
the words an old man signed:
be - came his ep - i - taph:

"For my chil - dren."

1.   2., 3.   Fine

(Spoken:) And the legs were shaped with his hands

and the top made of oak - en wood,

and the chil-dren that sat a-round this great ta-ble touched it

with their laugh-ter.   Ah, _ and that was good.

D.C. al Fine

(Instrumental)

NO LIMIT

Words and Music by NEIL DIAMOND
and RICHARD BENNETT

163

ONE GOOD LOVE

Words and Music by NEIL DIAMOND
and GARY NICHOLSON

It took a while __ for me to know
I fol-lowed all ____ life's pleas-ures

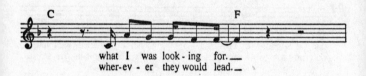

what I was look-ing for. __
wher-ev- er they would lead. __

And ev- 'ry heart __ I've __ ev- er known
But some-one I ____ can __ treas- ure

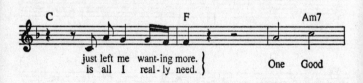

just left me want-ing more. }
is all I real - ly need. }

One   Good

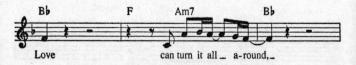

Love   can turn it all __ a-round, __

165

take hold _ of a rest - less heart

and lead it back to sol- id ground.

You can search the world _ for hap-pi-ness

and nev-er get _____ e - nough, _

when all you real-ly need _ to find _ is

D.C. al Coda

One Good ____ Love.

CODA

One Good Love can take you to the light.

With just one touch you can for-get a thou - sand empty nights.

You can search the world for hap-pi - ness and nev-er get e-nough, when all you real-ly need to find is One Good Love.

ON THE ROBERT E. LEE
from the Motion Picture THE JAZZ SINGER

Words and Music by
NEIL DIAMOND and GILBERT BECAUD

And have-n't you no-ticed, de-spite what it seems?___ You can't de-ny it's you and I a-lone. May-be spend my life just work-in' the land, may-be liv-in' from day to day.___ But I'm free to-night in New Or-leans;_ if I like it, I just might stay!

D.S. al Fine

ON THE WAY TO THE SKY

Words and Music by NEIL DIAMOND
and CAROLE BAYER SAGER

Country Waltz

I'm back on my feet a-gain, out on the street a-gain look-ing for love ___ On The Way To The Sky. ___ Some peo-ple mov-ing up, some peo-ple stand-ing still, some hold their hand out, and some peo-ple nev-er will. Lov-ers and li-ars con-sumed by the fires ___ of too man-y

172

ONCE IN A WHILE

Words and Music by
NEIL DIAMOND

Slowly and gently, in 2

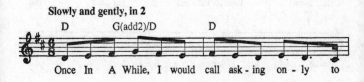

Once In A While, I would call ask - ing on - ly to

find you there.   Once In A While, I would

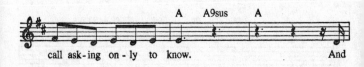

call ask - ing on - ly to know.   And

once you were mine long a - go when the eve - ning was

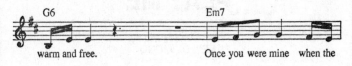

warm and free.   Once you were mine   when the

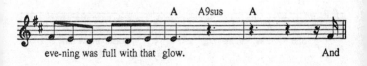

eve-ning was full with that glow.   And

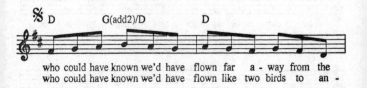

who could have known we'd have flown far   a - way from the
who could have known we'd have flown like two birds   to   an -

way we were,   know-ing the way we were __
oth-er place,   on-ly   to find our space __

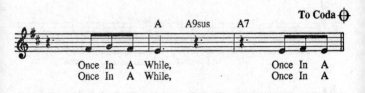

Once In A While,   Once In A
Once In A While,   Once In A

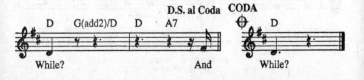

While?   And   While?

PLAY ME

Words and Music by
NEIL DIAMOND

She was morn-ing and I was night time. I
one day woke up to find her ly-in' be-
side my bed.   I soft-ly said, "Come
take me." ____   For
I've ____ been lone-ly, in ____ need of
So ____ it was that I ____ came to
some-one ____ as though I'd done some-one
tra-vel up-on ____ a road that was

wrong some - where, _____ but I don't know where.
thorned and nar - row. _____ An - oth - er place,

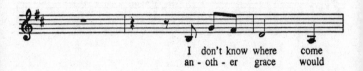

I don't know where come
an - oth - er grace would

late - ly. }
save me. }

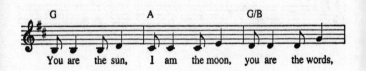

You are the sun, I am the moon, you are the words,

I am the tune: Play Me. __

Song she sang to me,

song she brang to me, words that rang in me,

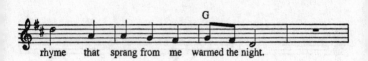

G

rhyme that sprang from me warmed the night.

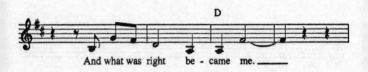

D

And what was right be - came me. ____

G   A

You are the sun, I am the moon,

G/B   A7/C#   D

you are the words, I am the tune: Play_ Me._

Dsus   D   Dsus   D.S. al Fine

(Instrumental)

OPEN WIDE THESE PRISON DOORS

Words and Music by
NEIL DIAMOND and STEWART HARRIS

Moderately slow

Tied by love ___ to you, ___
You were al - ways car - ing,

but I was tied ___ too strong. ___
al - ways warm ___ and kind. ___

Still, I'm a - fraid ___ of know-in'
But that was long ___ a - go ___

what leav - in' means. ___
when love was blind. ___

I know I lived ___ for you ___
And I don't want ___ to hurt you

in all I tried ___ to do. ___
the way that I've ___ been hurt. ___

You were the keep - er of ___ my dreams. ___
But if I stay, ___ I'll lose ___ my mind. ___

and set me free.

Time _____ is al - ways mov - ing

while we're here _____ stand-ing _____ still. _____

I'll love you e - ven though _____ I'm leav - ing.

And may-be I al - ways will. _____

PORCUPINE PIE

Words and Music by
NEIL DIAMOND

Moderately

Por - cu - pine Pie, Por - cu - pine Pie, Por - cu - pine

Pie, Va - nil - la soup, —

a dou - ble scoop, — please. No,

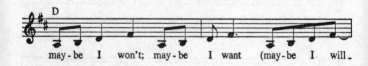

may - be I won't; may - be I want (may - be I will —

—) the tut - ti fruit —

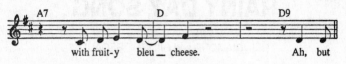

with fruit-y bleu__ cheese. Ah, but

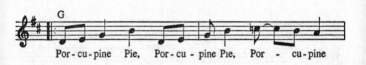

Por-cu-pine Pie, Por-cu-pine Pie, Por __ cu-pine

Pie, { don't let ____ it get ____ on your
{ it weaves __ it's way ____ through my

jeans.   I know   it__ sounds __
dreams.   And I   do be-lieve __

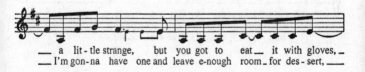

__ a lit-tle strange,   but you got to   eat__ it with gloves, __
__ I'm gon-na have one and leave e-nough room_ for des-sert, __

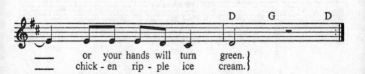

__   or your hands will turn   green. }
__   chick-en rip-ple ice   cream. }

RAINY DAY SONG

Words and Music by
NEIL DIAMOND and GILBERT BECAUD

Can you hear my Rain-y Day _ Song,
It's just an-oth-er Rain-y Day _ Song,
Can you hear that Rain-y Day _ Song?

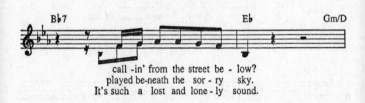

call-in' from the street be - low?
played be-neath the sor - ry sky.
It's such a lost and lone-ly sound.

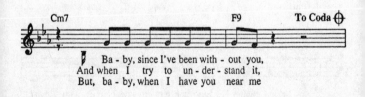

Ba - by, since I've been with-out you,
And when I try to un-der-stand it,
But, ba-by, when I have you near me

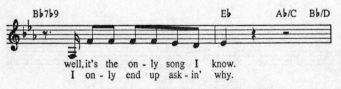

well, it's the on-ly song I know.
I on-ly end up ask-in' why.

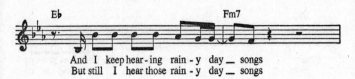

And I keep hear-ing rain-y day ___ songs
But still I hear those rain-y day ___ songs

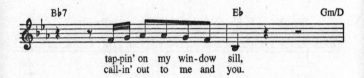

tap-pin' on my win-dow sill,
call-in' out to me and you.

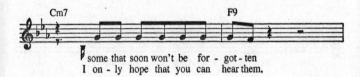

some that soon won't be for-got-ten
I on-ly hope that you can hear them,

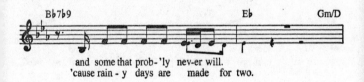

and some that prob-'ly nev-er will.
'cause rain-y days are made for two.

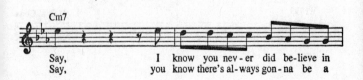

Say, I know you nev-er did be-lieve in
Say, you know there's al-ways gon-na be a

rain-bows.
rain-bow.

But
And

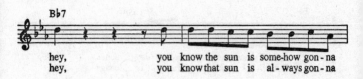

Bb7

hey,   you know the sun is some-how gon-na
hey,   you know that sun is al-ways gon-na

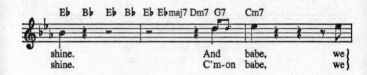

Eb   **Bb**   **Eb**   **Bb**   **Eb**   **Ebmaj7**   **Dm7**   **G7**   **Cm7**

shine.   And   babe,   we }
shine.   C'm-on babe,   we }

F9

on-ly have to look and we can find it,

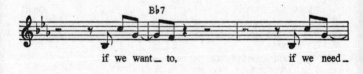

Bb7

if we want __ to,   if we need __

Bb7b9

1.   **2.**   **D.C. al Coda**

__ to.

CODA
⊕   **Rubato**
Bb7b9   **Eb**

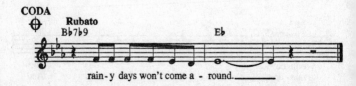

rain-y days won't come a - round.____

SEPTEMBER MORN

Words and Music by
NEIL DIAMOND and GILBERT BECAUD

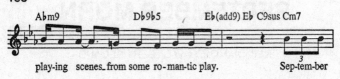

playing scenes from some romantic play. Sep-tem-ber

morn-ings still can make me feel that way.

Look at what you've done. Why, you've be-come a grown-up girl.

I still can hear you cry-ing in the cor-ner of your room.

And look how ___ far we've come: so

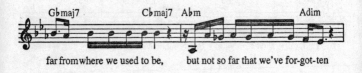

far from where we used to be, but not so far that we've for-got-ten

how it was ___ be-fore. Sep-tem-ber Morn. Do you re-

mem - ber ___ how we danced ___ that night a - way?

Two lov-ers play-ing scenes ___ from some ro-man-tic play.

Sep-tem-ber morn-ings still can make me feel that

way. Sep-tem-ber Morn. We

danced un-til the night be-came a brand new day. Two lov-ers

play-ing scenes ___ from some ro-man-tic play. Sep-tem-ber

morn-ings still can make me feel that way.

RED, RED WINE

Words and Music by
NEIL DIAMOND

Slow Country beat

Red, Red Wine, _____ go to my head, make me for-get that I still need her so. Red, Red Wine, _____ it's up to you. All I can do, I've done; but mem-'ries won't go. No, mem-'ries won't go.

I'd have thought that with time thoughts of her would leave my head. I was wrong, and I find just one thing makes me for . get. Red, Red Wine, stay close to me. Don't let me be a-lone. It's tear-ing a-part my blue, blue

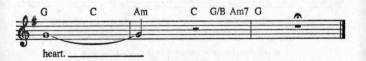

heart.

REMINISCE FOR
A WHILE

Words and Music by NEIL DIAMOND
and RAUL MALO

ROSEMARY'S WINE

Words and Music by
NEIL DIAMOND

And her eyes hurt the way they do, Al-most like they'd seen, Al-most like they knew. And her words, soft as they could be, tied me to her soul and could-n't set me free. And the night drink

that held us in its arms, it held us once a -
the sweet-ness of her soul, and drink it once a -

SAY MAYBE

Words and Music by
NEIL DIAMOND

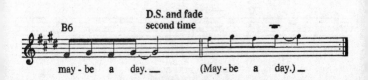

SIGNS

Words and Music by
NEIL DIAMOND

Moderately

Signs _ that burn like shoot - ing stars ____

that pass a - cross _ the night - time skies, _

they reach out __ in their mys - tic lan-guage

for us to read _ be - tween _ the lines.

Some are born who would de - fy them,

oth-ers still who would de - ny

them.   Signs.

Signs   like   mo-ments   hung ___ sus-pend-ed, ___

ech-oes   just   be-neath ___ the   heart, ___

speak in   voic-es   half ___ re-mem-bered ___

and   half-re-mem-bered   play ___ their   part. ___

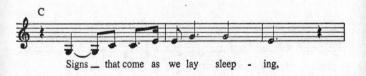

Signs ___ that come as   we   lay   sleep - ing,

left   be-hind   for   our ___ keep -

200

ing.   **C**   Signs.

C7

Sail __ a - long,   *(Instrumental)*

3

sail a - long the reefs __ and the coves __ in - side

F   *3*   **C7**

your soul.   Sail a - long. __

(Instrumental)   Sail a - long   in   search __

3   **F**

__ of a star that you __ can hold.

G

And we jour - ney far   to where that __

C — star may lead to. D

(lead to.) (Instrumental)

D
Signs _ that whis-per in ___ the ___ dreams _ of ___

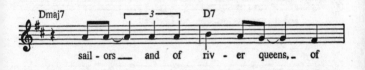

Dmaj7 — 3 — D7
sail - ors ___ and of riv - er queens, _ of

G
pau-pers and of men with means. _

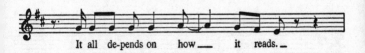

It all de-pends on how ___ it reads. _

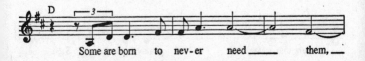

D — 3 —
Some are born to nev-er need ___ them, _

202

oth-ers still who nev-er read ___ them. ___

___ Signs. Sail a - long, ___

(Instrumental) sail a - long the reefs.

___ and the coves ___ in-side your ___ soul.

Sail a - long, ___ *(Instrumental)*

sail a-long in search ___ of a star that you can hold.

And we jour- ney far to

where that star ___ may lead to. Signs.

SHILO

Words and Music by
NEIL DIAMOND

Moderately

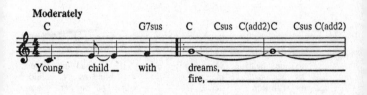

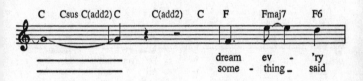

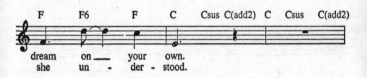

SKYBIRD
from JONATHAN LIVINGSTON SEAGULL,
the film by Hall Bartlett

Words and Music by
NEIL DIAMOND

Sky - bird ____ make your sail, and eve - ry heart will know ___ of the tale. *(Instrumental)*

Song - bird ____ make your tune, for none may sing it just ___ as you do.

Spoken: { 1. And head for the farthest shore.
{ 2. And make your song be heard.

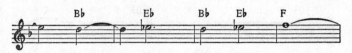

Look at the way _____

_____ I glide, caught on the wind's la -

- zy tide. _____ Sweet - ly how it sings.

Ral - ly each

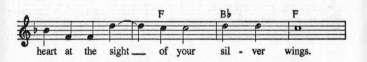

heart at the sight _____ of your sil - ver wings.

Sky - bird,

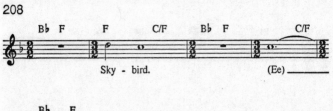

Sky - bird.　　　　　　　(Ee) _____

_____　Night - bird _____ find your way,

for　　none　may

know　it　just _____ as　you　may.

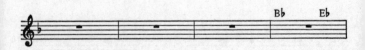

Play 3 times

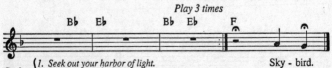

Spoken: {
1. *Seek out your harbor of light.*
2. *Let your song be heard.*
3. *Rally each heart at the sight of your silver wings.*
}

Sky - bird.

SOOLAIMON

Words and Music by
NEIL DIAMOND

Come, she — come say, _____
Bring home — my name _____

ride _____
on _____

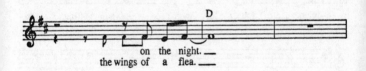

on the night. —
the wings of a flea. —

Sun be-come day, _____
Wind in the plain, _____

day _____
dance _____

SOLITARY MAN

Words and Music by
NEIL DIAMOND

SONG SUNG BLUE

Words and Music by
NEIL DIAMOND

SONGS OF LIFE
from THE JAZZ SINGER

Words and Music by NEIL DIAMOND
and GILBERT BECAUD

Gently and smoothly

Songs __ Of Life, they ring from qui-et

stee-ples to dis-tant val-leys a-long the

hill-sides of lov-ers' hearts, of lov-ers'

hearts. Come

sing ____ your Songs Of Life, ____
sing ____ my Songs Of Life ____

STARGAZER

Words and Music by
NEIL DIAMOND

Star - gaz - er,

you with your head in the heav - ens, you'll

nev-er get __ by __ walk-in' that high __ off the ground.

__ Moon _____ dream-
Star - gaz -

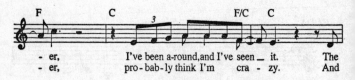

- er, I've been a-round, and I've seen __ it. The
- er, pro - bab - ly think I'm cra - zy. And

G7

high-er you get,__ the hard-er they let__ you__ down.
you have-n't heard__ one sin-gle word__ I've__ said.__

C   F   C7   F

__   You pay your dues__
__   Now I don't want__

C

it seems for-ev- er.
to burst your bub- ble,

G7

And if__ you're clev- er,
but you__ got trou- ble.

N.C.

you may be in for a while, then you're__
Don't you know the high-er the top, the long-

C

__ out of style. Hey
- er the drop. Hey   Star - gaz-

F   C   F7   C   F7   C

er.

STONES

Words and Music by
NEIL DIAMOND

Lord - y, child, ___
You and me, ___

a good day's com - in', ___
a time for plant - ing. ___

and I'll be there
You and me, ___

to let the sun ___ in. ___ And
a har - vest grant - ing ___ the

be - in' lost ___
ev - 'ry prayer ___ ev - er prayed

is worth the com - in'
for just two wild flow'rs in that

home.}
grow.} La la la la ___ la la

la la la ___ on Stones.

THE STORY OF MY LIFE

Words and Music by
NEIL DIAMOND

Slowly

The Sto - ry Of My Life
Life,

is ver - y plain to read.
and ev - 'ry word is true.

It starts the day you came
Each chap - ter sings your name;

and ends the day you leave.
each page be - gins with you.

The Sto - ry Of My Life
It's the sto - ry of our times

224

SWEET CAROLINE

Words and Music by
NEIL DIAMOND

226

E7   %A

long?   Hands,
        Warm,

A6   E7

touch-in' hands, }
touch-in' warm, }   reach-in' out,

D

touch-in' me,   touch - in'

E7   D/F♯ E/G♯   A

you._____ (Instrumental) Sweet Car - o - line,

D

___ (Instrumental) good times nev – er seemed so

E7   D/F♯ E/G♯   A

good.   (Instrumental) I've been in - clined_

D   To Coda ⊕

___ (Instrumental) to be – lieve_ they nev – er

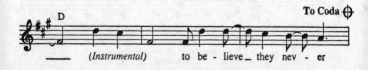

STREET LIFE

Words and Music by
NEIL DIAMOND

Moderately

Hey, let me show you the Street _ Life.
Say, let me show you the night _ life.

Hey, let me show you the finks, _ the punks, the judge, the
Say, let me show you the queens, _ the dudes, the class, the

junk - ie. Stay _ close to me for a while, for a
crudes, the folks _ that in - hab - it the night. Let me

while, for a while. } *(Instrumental)*
set it right. }

E7

Say boy, you got to get street-
I'm gon - na give you my warn-

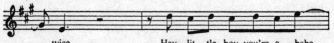

- wise.   Hey, lit - tle boy, you're a babe _
- ing.   I'm gon - na tell you the street's _

— in arms. Stay out of harm's — way right — here with
— a-live, the sound of jive; you've just — ar-rived.

me for a while, for a while, for a while.)
Try it for size for a while, for a while.)

(Instrumental)

E7

Street Life, hell — in the cit-y.

You got to real-ly watch out for that Street Life. Say, —

— it ain't pret-ty, you got to know your way

a-round, or some-how you might get hurt, get hurt, — get hurt.

To Coda ⊕

(Instrumental)

D.C. al Coda

CODA
⊕

(Instrumental)

SUMMERLOVE
from THE JAZZ SINGER

Words and Music by NEIL DIAMOND
and GILBERT BECAUD

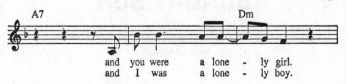

and you were a lone - ly girl.
and I was a lone - ly boy.

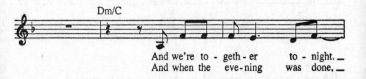

And we're to - geth - er to - night. __
And when the eve - ning was done, __

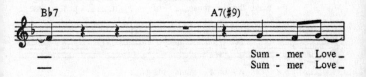

__ Sum - mer Love __
__ Sum - mer Love __

1. (D.C.)

__ made it right.
__ made us one.

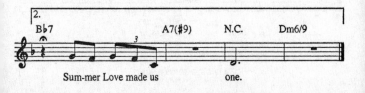

2.

Sum-mer Love made us one.

SUNDAY SUN

Words and Music by
NEIL DIAMOND

234

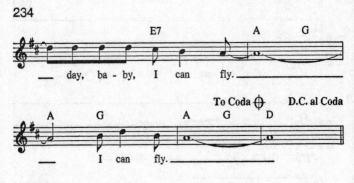

day, ba - by, I can fly. ____

To Coda ⊕ **D.C. al Coda**

I can fly. ____

CODA
⊕

Hey Sun - day ___ Sun, ___

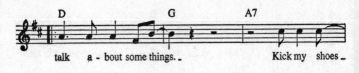

let's go walk - in', and ___ we'll

talk a - bout some things. ___ Kick my shoes ___

___ off, and ___ we'll dream a - bout some dreams.

Repeat and Fade

G   A

Come on Sun - day Sun, ___ we'll

YOU MAKE IT FEEL LIKE CHRISTMAS

Words and Music by
NEIL DIAMOND

Slowly

Look at   us now,   part of   it all.   In
Lov-ers   in love,   just like   we were.

spite of   it all, we're still ___ a-round.
Be-ing a-part's a lone- ___ -ly sound.

When peo - ple ask   how   we stay   to-geth-er,

I say   you nev - er let ___ me down.   And

You Make It Feel ___ Like Christ - mas

e - ven when things go wrong. ___

I hear the sound of Christ - mas in your song ___

all year long. Look at the sun

shin-ing on me. No-where could be a bet - ter place.

Lov - ers in love, that's what we are. I

reach for that star out there ___ in space. 'Cause

You Make It Feel ___ Like Christ - mas

e-ven when things go wrong.

I hear the sound of Christ-mas in your song

all year long.

Sleep-y we are, but hap-py to-geth-er.

Sounds of for-ev-er greet the day. So

wake up the kids. Put on some tea.

Light up the tree; it's Christ-mas day. Yeah,

TALKING OPTIMIST BLUES
(Good Day Today)

Words and Music by
NEIL DIAMOND and GRETCHEN PETERS

Moderately fast

F

I got wor- ries by the ton; ___
Bills and pills and for- mer wives, ___
Pulled my back and wrecked my car. ___

C7

get- tin' can- cer's on- ly one. ___
past mis- takes ___ and for- mer lives. ___
Girl-friend stole ___ my V. C. R. ___

F

O- ver- taxed and al- i- mo- nied,
Bank ac- count is o- ver- drawn, ___
Let- ter came from *Six- ty Min- utes;*

Bb

tired of eat- in' fried ba- lo- ney.
out of Pro- zac, hair- line's ___ gone. ___
say they wan- na put me in ___ it.

F

I got bur- dens on my shoul- ders,
Hear- ing voic- es in my head; ___
Tell me my ca- reer just died. ___

C

dy- ing young or grow- in' old- er.
say I should -'ve stayed in bed.
Years a- go I might -'ve cried.

TENNESSEE MOON

Words and Music by NEIL DIAMOND
and DENNIS MORGAN

Moderately fast

Hol - ly-wood don't do___ what it once___ could do.
Touched down and she stole___ my heart right___ a -

way.
Be - gan to think for the

write me a song___ be-fore noon.___
first time I___ might___ stay.___

So I packed my dust - y bags___ one night,
And when I heard that lone - some whis - tle moan,___

grabbed an old gui - tar,___ and I
knew I'd fi - n'lly

caught a red - eye flight. }
found my way back home. }

In search___

___ of a dream___ un - der - neath___ the Ten - nes-see

Moon, ____ I ____ fell in love ____ to an old ____ Hank Wil - liams tune. ____ { Makes me } { And I }

1. wonder: is it the same moon Hank played un - der?

2. wonder: is it the same moon Hank stood un - der when he sang ____ a - bout jam - ba - la - ya and be - in' lone - some e - nough to cry? ____ And I can hear ____ the ech - oes in the sounds of his ____ gui - tar. And his words still paint a pic - ture in ____ my ____ heart. Yeah, in search ____

THANK THE LORD
FOR THE NIGHT TIME

Words and Music by
NEIL DIAMOND

Moderate Rock beat

Day - time turns me off,____ and I don't mean
Talk a - bout plans now, ba - by, I got

may - be. Nine - to - five ____ ain't
plen - ty. Noth-ing ev - er seems to turn ____

tak-in' me where I'm bound.
____ out the way it should.

When it's done, I run out to see my
Talk a - bout mon - ey, girl, I ain't got

ba - by. We get
an - y. Seems like

groov - in' when the sun goes
just one time I'm feel - in'

down.}
good.}
I Thank The Lord For The Night Time

to for-get the day. ___

A day of up... up - tight ___ time,

ba - by, chase it a - way.

I get re - lax - a - tion. ___

It's a time to groove. ___

I Thank The Lord For The Night Time

I thank the Lord for you.

WIN THE WORLD

Words and Music by NEIL DIAMOND
and SUSAN LONGACRE

Moderately slow

I nev-er no-ticed when you changed your
should have been me there for all of those

hair, just an-oth-er of those mo-ments
times. It would have been me there

I was on-ly half there. When
if I knew the signs. When

you wore that red dress that was cut up to
you wore that red dress, how could I know

here, I nev-er no-ticed
then you'd wear it for me once

you were wear-ing a tear. I was
but nev-er wear it a-gain?

YESTERDAY'S SONGS

Words and Music by
NEIL DIAMOND

Moderately

Yes-ter-day's Songs _ don't stay a-round_long,_ not
Yes-ter-day's Songs _ don't seem to be - long._ They're

much an - y - more. _____
here, and they're gone. _____

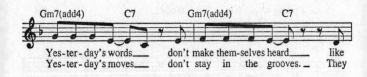

Yes-ter-day's words___ don't make them-selves heard____ like
Yes-ter-day's moves___ don't stay in the grooves._ They

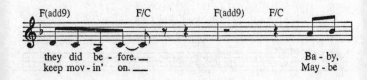

they did be - fore. _ Ba - by,
keep mov-in' on. _ May - be

yes - ter - day's _ blues _____ may be
yes - ter - day's _ rhyme _____ was for

yes - ter - day's __ news, _____ but the
yes - ter - day's __ time, _____ and the

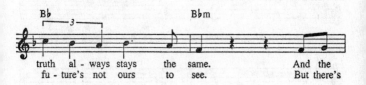

truth al - ways stays the same. And the
fu - ture's not ours to see. But there's

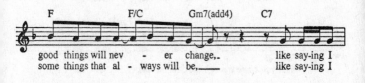

good things will nev - er change,_ like say-ing I
some things that al - ways will be,_ like say-ing I

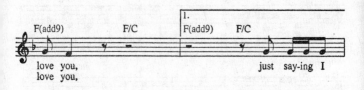

love you, just say-ing I
love you,

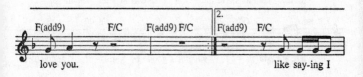

love you. like say-ing I

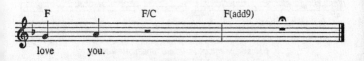

love you.

YOU DON'T BRING ME FLOWERS

Words by NEIL DIAMOND,
MARILYN BERGMAN and ALAN BERGMAN
Music by NEIL DIAMOND

Slowly and freely

You Don't Bring Me Flow-ers; you don't sing me love songs.

You hard-ly talk to me an-y-more

when you come through the door at the end of the day.

I re-mem-ber when you could-n't wait to love me,

used to hate to leave me. Now af-ter lov-in' me

late at night when it's good for you and you're

feel-in' all right, well, you just roll o-ver, and you

YOU GOT TO ME

Words and Music by
NEIL DIAMOND

Moderate Gospel beat

Ma - ma told me that some - day it would
Used to slip through ev - 'ry girl's hands like

hap - pen.
wa - ter.
But
There

she nev - er said that it would hap - pen like
nev - er was one who could ev - er tie me

this.
down.
Pa - pa said, "Look out, some
Straight a - head and stead -

girl - 'll catch you nap - pin'.
- y as Gi - bral - tar,

Some lit - tle girl will get to you with her
till you brought me tum - bl - in' to the

GUITAR CHORD FRAMES

This guitar chord reference includes 120 commonly used chords. For a more complete guide to guitar chords, see "THE PAPERBACK CHORD BOOK" (HL00702009).

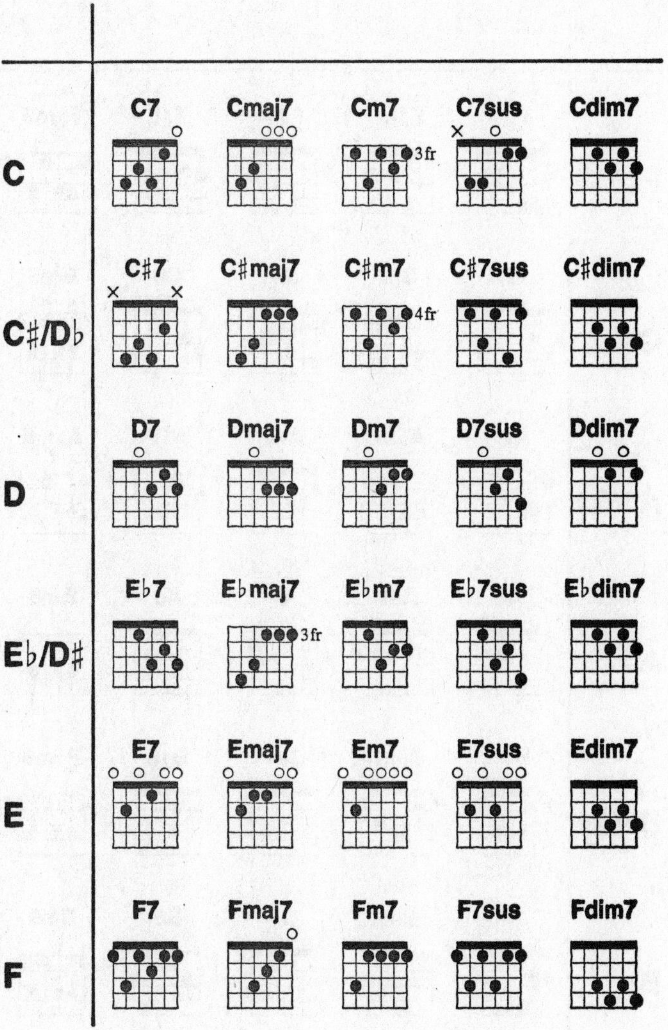
C
C7
Cmaj7
Cm7
3fr
C7sus
Cdim7
C♯/D♭
C♯7
C♯maj7
C♯m7
4fr
C♯7sus
C♯dim7
D
D7
Dmaj7
Dm7
D7sus
Ddim7
E♭/D♯
E♭7
E♭maj7
3fr
E♭m7
E♭7sus
E♭dim7
E
E7
Emaj7
Em7
E7sus
Edim7
F
F7
Fmaj7
Fm7
F7sus
Fdim7

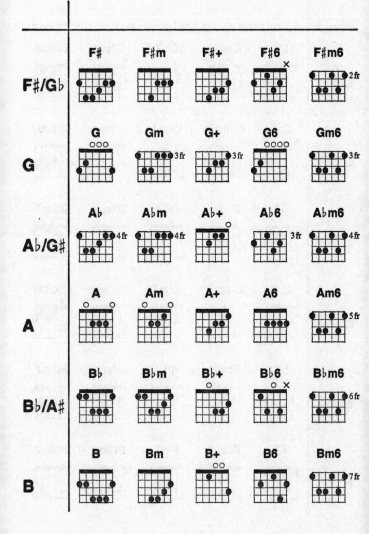

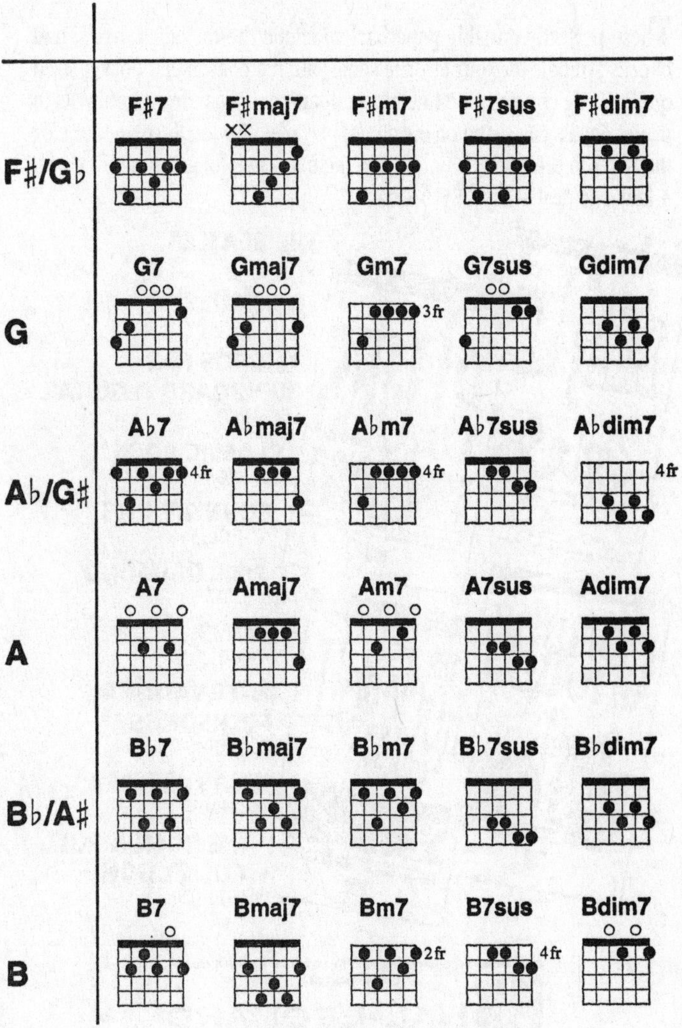
F♯/G♭
F♯7
F♯maj7
F♯m7
F♯7sus
F♯dim7
G
G7
Gmaj7
Gm7
3fr
G7sus
Gdim7
A♭/G♯
A♭7
4fr
A♭maj7
A♭m7
4fr
A♭7sus
A♭dim7
4fr
A
A7
Amaj7
Am7
A7sus
Adim7
B♭/A♯
B♭7
B♭maj7
B♭m7
B♭7sus
B♭dim7
B
B7
Bmaj7
Bm7
2fr
B7sus
4fr
Bdim7

THE PAPERBACK SONGS SERIES

These perfectly portable paperbacks include the melodies, lyrics, and chords symbols for your favorite songs, all in a convenient, pocket-sized book. Using concise, one-line music notation, anyone from hobbyists to professionals can strum on the guitar, play melodies on the piano, or sing the lyrics to great songs. Books also include a helpful guitar chord chart. A fantastic deal – only $5.95 each!

THE BEATLES
00702008

THE BLUES
00702014

CHORDS FOR KEYBOARD & GUITAR
00702009

CLASSIC ROCK
00310058

COUNTRY HITS
00702013

NEIL DIAMOND
00702012

HYMNS
00240103

INTERNATIONAL FOLKSONGS
00240104

ELVIS PRESLEY
00240102

THE ROCK & ROLL COLLECTION
00702020

FOR MORE INFORMATION, SEE YOUR LOCAL MUSIC DEALER,
OR WRITE TO:

HAL•LEONARD®
CORPORATION
7777 W. BLUEMOUND RD. P.O. BOX 13819 MILWAUKEE, WI 53213

Prices, availability and contents subject to change without notice.
Some products may not be available outside the U.S.A.